Love to God of the Mountains

Namita Ambadas Nanda

BookLeaf
Publishing

India | USA | UK

Made with ❤ on the BookLeaf Publishing Platform
www.bookleafpub.in
www.bookleafpub.com

Dedicated to the memory of my Father

Ambadas Nandagaoli

and Mumma, who gave me the gift of dreams
and the ability to realize them.

Acknowledgement

I'm extremely grateful to BookLeaf Publishing for giving me a platform to publish my poetries.

This book is dedicated to my Father whom I had lost in Covid. His blessing and praises kept me moving on.

I cannot begin to express my thanks to my best friends who were appreciating my drafted work. I would like to extend my sincere thanks to my Family and my lovely Son especially. I would also like to extend my sincere thanks to the God of mountains—Lord Khandoba.

Preface

The experiences in life, good or bad, bring out hidden talents in oneself. When we experience a rough phase, we start doing those things which give us peace of mind and where we can express our inner self, our fears, unexpressed thoughts with no filters. Poetry is one such blessing.

This collection of poetries is an exploration of moments of Love, Infatuation, un-quenched Desires, Loneliness and Separations. In the poetries you shall find the delicate tenderness of love's first bloom, the burning intensity of longing, and the painful silence that follows the breaking of bond. Understanding love and its all forms is both a blessing and lesson. Perhaps reading these poems you shall find that you are not alone in your own journey through them. The author seeks blessing from every God's particle for her first attempt.

1. Losing you!

How do love and revenge taste like...?
It's insatiable if it's deep inside the heart and
left unexpressed...
This racking pain of not having you in my
arms..keeps coming to the surface...
I ran afar...yet it makes its way to all my
hiding places..
Humiliates me... makes me feel like lost war
soldier living in solace!

Looking at you every time... the flame of love
and revenge ignites..
That feeling of vengeance poisons my sensory
neurites..

The scalding pain of losing you and deceit..

Shall seek justice in vain...

Till the heart is repaired and sanity of
emotion is attained!

2. As we grew up…

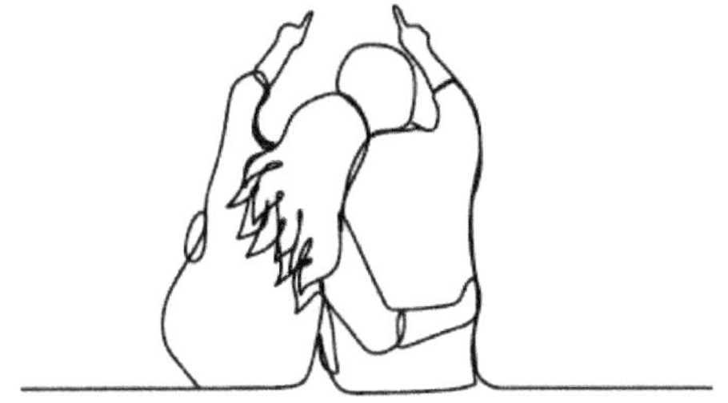

Lying below the sky on the grasses…checking
on the aeroplanes..
Dreaming to be a pilot in sunny summers.
Soaring above the mountain ranges..

Catching dandelions.. teasing caterpillars and
climbing trees.. fighting with twigs ..
Impersonated to be henchmen..

Skimming stones across the pond… On one
go..
collecting pebbles and shells…
Sailing our hopes through the ocean..

Discover and exploring the secret places in
neighborhoods..
Did a hundred treasure hunts...having a
Spiffing bottle cans collection..

Wandering the night skies. Bottling the
fireflies.. Prattling the stories of ghosts and
magical things..
Semblance to be a Batman..

So many so many things we wished we
aspired we had pride for...
Must be lost somewhere as we grew up
That innocence wanting we threw up..

So many things so many things we were
happy about..
Got lost somewhere as we became mature..
That impromptu life of adventures has
disappeared.. !

3. Barren Heart

It feels to be a discourse from long back..
While it was only yesterday.. that you have
left me...

Now it's dark in here..seems it's deserted and I
walked to a long tunnel that never ceases..
With my withered heart and wailing eyes
which want pain to unleash..

It feels to be a forever thing now...that I cry
when it rains..
The barren heart delights for a moment of his
memories and you are not here..! That
delightful feeling wanes..

As it was only yesterday.. that you have left
me..

The long walk in this dark tunnel shall be
long till I obliviate..

And God had had enough
entertained..playing my life like a string
marionette
And it feels to be forever thing that I have
been broke, left and played...

Paying for falling in love..being honest to you
and submitted..
As it was only yesterday.. that you have left
me!

4. Attraction

I took up the brush and painted a beautiful
picture of him..
His beauty is in hues of his heart that I see...

As there lies the wisdom with brilliance in an
artistic mind..
A soulful man who stands for every mankind..

His igniting vision and husky appearance
make him a rare one in his clan..
And Hey! Beardo..whenever you are around I
capture your glance..

That is the time when it feels my heart is
stolen. . .
I envy the thought that he will be for another
woman.

It's hard to tell how much I have fallen..
His every morph is tattooed in my bosom.
His calmness like a cobalt and anger was like
fiery red..

His possessiveness was like orange
shades..priceless is his crimson color hugs..
He is white when he patronises me.. He is
black when he sacrifices to every degree..
I wish I could paint down all his facets on a
canvas..
And kept it locked forever in my secret vault.

5. Love to God of Mountains

I was loving you at dusk and at the darkest of
nights..
Waking up with you in the brightest of
daylights..

Rushing to you like wildfire on your
command in the summer heats..
Get distant like a star in a faraway galaxy
when you feel guilty..

Because I loosened up and tied only to you..
Still in love with you and pretended I am not.

I cared about every emotion and unable to
unravel..
While you oscillated between we and me! Our
relationship tangled..

This is no more a rope that will lead to each
other's end...
It has become a maze that nowhere sends..!

You have become that mountain top that
never leans..
While I have been that cloud that settled by
you or rains!

तुम उस विशाल पहाड़ के शिखर हो जो झुकता
कहाँ,

और मैं उन बादलों की तरह रहा, जो तुम्हारी
पनाहों पर बरस जाता रहा।

6. Self actualisation

When I was looking for love outside..
The whole of it was inside ..
It's that I never looked in the mirror with that
eye..
I have been looking at you ..wanting it..my
whole life..

And wished that our hands joined in prayers
together...
While the peace was not in the mind
whatsoever..
We have been judging each other forever..
And love was not as it was foretold in
fairytale literature.

Eventually, I realized. When the countdown
of life begins tik-tok backwards to
non-existent..
And when I saw the mirror image of LoVE is
EVoL...
That we evolve as time grows and life
shortens.

We won't be perfect from the beginning.
We have to believe and trust while unfolding..
The life..and accept...else we left insatiate and
discontent at the end.

7. Helpless heart

You were there standing on the other side of
this river...
And I learnt crossing it's hard and reaching
you is harder..

Your voice was not reachable... and I gotta
feel that I am drowning to its depth..
I shall be down to death bed....
and would be a complete wreck..

Now I need someone to breathe me back to
life..

Because I will no longer seeing your sight..
Because there shall no longer be your kisses.
And there will be no insane reaches...

So..I will be needing stitches...

And there you are.. will be standing on the
other side of the river..

And I learnt crossing is hard and reaching
you is even harder..

Because there will no longer be your arms
around..
Because there shall be no warmth. Surround.
And there will be no more your aiding hand..

So...I will be needing a mend..

And I need someone to breathe me back to
life!
And I need to reach your cliff..

8. Midnight Romance

On a plenilune night.. You were desired by
whole of me..
Like the moon illuminated the sky as far as
one can see..

The rush in my adrenaline as I see you.. leads
me to have you..
and when I touch you ..it feels like I own you..
I rule you and I submit me to you..

On this full moon night.. You are desired by
whole of me..

Like the night fire has a fervent desire to
embrace everything it sees..

Your presence is soothing like a winter breeze
and first rain..
When you cuddle me, it feels like whiskey
poured in an icy Glencairn..

It's midnight and we have each other ..
Love songs, candlelit, the look on your eyes
and kisses forever.

On this lunar night.. we are desired in whole
of each other.
Like the midnight sky had enclasped every
celestial body visible from the earth.

9. Your Happy places

Stranger! When I met you, you were just a
stranger...
You read my eyes and I read your heart....
We exchange glances sometimes ..
while we didn't speak..admiring each other!

Surrendered to our helpless hearts, we met at
your happy places!

The heart beckons us to complete. What was
untold on faces!

Mind quelled the wishes we had before...but
subdued fire flashes..

The caged bird took the flight outside..
It strolls on to your happy places...

It breathed..it soared high..it filled her lungs
with fresh breezes..
It flew high with you and lived the moment
she seized..

Though destiny wished for different
universes..

However we shall time travel again to your
happy places!

10. Acceptance to real life.

When you shall return..Maybe I won't be
there..standing!
There would be no more me on your romantic
ending!

It mayhap that we both are destined to be
apart...
And Time has come now to depart!

Sometimes we take wrong paths on the right
track for meeting a beautiful tragedy!
And people say..that's how our karma cycle
fixes its past life malady.

We accept the destiny given to us like the Holy
water..
We lay down to death with the belief that
prayers shall be answered!

So, you and I had the consortium for only a
little while.
Hence..we had love, we shall ruin, we shall
move on..and..thrive..!

11. No strings attached and no threads torn....

On a breezy winter..near some lake..we walk
past a boat and fisherman's hope...

We climbed down the siltstone arch..we
looked for a rope..

We met a few children and some swans..both
eloped..

We sat by the lake..I blabber ..he listened..
He talks about himself and I lippen...

He sang to me..I sang along..the song was
from some melodious band..

Holding hands we crossed the damp terrain..
No strings attached, no threads being torn!?

Lie ahead of us are..destinations
ahead..behind was a day of gem!
we had a zest of the feel and could have never
let it run!

Alas! No strings attached..no threads being
torn!

12. Together

Winter's night and snow had covered the mountains around...

We are buried in the warm quilt and frost froze the window's background...

I lie my head on your shoulder and the beats of your heart are louder than the wind's blustering sounds...
This night..with you, for sure is going to be spellbound!!!

Rush and hush of our lives..we are so duty-bound!
I didn't get you ..you couldn't catch me around...

Baby! Here is our moment to compound..!
The vacuum of our life needs to be disbarred..now let the love be filled around.
This night..with you for sure is going to be spellbound!

13. Travel with me...

Travel with me again to the Lands of Gods...
Let's walk past.. crossing those rocky cairns
we built last time..
Reaching the seven mountains; near the Holy
Shrine..
By the lake we chanted the Ek Onkar
rhymes..

Travel with me again to the River chosen for
repenting souls...
Let's walk past.. losing sight of our differences
we built last time...
Reaching the flowing glaciers, cleanse the
stains of mind.
By the pious banks of rivers, we bowed to
that one Divine..

Travel with me again to the heavens of
angels..
Let's walk past.. exploring new destinations
we shall treasure for remembrance next time..

Reaching each other's heart; becoming better humankind...
By the pious hearts, we become the beacon of light.
Travel with me...........

14. You & I and this Old city

Starring skies... crescent moon...and this old city....
You and I; startles in the eyes... and it's raining past memories of confetti..

Old architecture of the city..old archives of us....and stealing glances in the evening twilight..

Starring skies ..crescent moon and alas! Our chaos plight.

Constellations above changing axes! I for next glances of you in excitement...

You and I; crystal lakes .....and its breezing winds at daylight..
Too many places to be with you but your hesitant heart is saying it's not right.

City didn't shambles..existed in timelessness...so the stars..moon..twilights and memories of You!

15. Wanderlust with you..

We met on the mountainside..we walked a
few miles in the starlight..
We caught a few fireflies on the way...for our
delight..

We sang songs with an antakshari vibe..
We faked smoke.. exhaling the cold breath
with a rolled hollow pipe..

We behaved like drunks and laughed all
night..

We were on a bus.. returning from our
training site..
You got down to visit your hometown at the
festival of lights..

I saw you going and going and..our journey
divides..

Our travelogue moments were happy and sad
now...

I miss our stupid talks and your silly vow..

I waited for you while lost memories played
in a loop..
Coming back was all I wished with all my
might..

With you were the best moments of my life!

16. Gumnaam sa pyar..

ज़िंदगी से चाहत रही कुछ और थी मेरी..
पन्नों में कहानी कुछ और दर्ज हो रही थी..
ज़िंदगी से चाहत रही कुछ और थी मेरी..
पन्नों में कहानी कुछ और दर्ज हो रही थी..
सबकी सब दुआएँ कुबूल हो रही थी
सिवा एक अर्ज़ जो मेरी जो खाली रह गयी थी।

इस बारिश की तरह मेरा प्यार भी बे-आमेज़िश
रहा..
बस उसे ही दुनिया की मंज़ूरी दिला ना पायी।
तुझसे फुर्कत सह भी न पायी..
तेरे नाम लेने की इजाज़त मुझे मिल भी न पायी।

पाक दिल को इजाज़त बस तुझसे मिले..
और ये कहानी तेरी मेरी बस यूँ ही हममें रह जाए..

जो चाहत रही कुछ और थी..मेरी..
दर्ज मेरे ग़ज़लों के पन्नों मे ज़िक्र हो तेरा,
ए बाला-तर..हम. गुमनामी में खो जाय।

17. Confession

कह दो ना प्यार ही था वो.. जो तूने मुझसे कहा था
वो एक दिन।
प्यार ही था जब तू बाहों में भर लिया करता था,
मुझसे मिल.. वो हर एक दिन।
मोहब्बत ही थी जो तुमसे दूर जाने पर उतना ही
कशिश दे रही है मुझे तेरे पास रहने की।

तेरे हाथों को अपने हाथो में लेकर.. कुछ भी न
कहने की।
वो मोहब्बत ही थी।
कहो...

मोहब्बत थी जिनमें मानदण्ड पार किये जा रहे थे,
दंगो में तुझसे मिलने जा रही थी, तेरी फ़िकर की
दुआ पढ़े जा रही थी।
वो मोहब्बत थी, वो सौदाई नहीं थी कोई बेवफाई
नहीं थी, कोई खुदगर्ज़ी नहीं, कोई दिल्लगी नहीं..
मेरे-हमारे प्यार की souvenir थी..
वो मोहब्बत ही थी..
कहो तुम वही थे जो, जिसको चाहा था, जिसने
मुझसे कहा था वो एक दिन..
कि मोहब्बत है।

18. Mera Anshian aur Tum

ज़्यादा क्या कहूं और क्या न कहूं...
तू होता मेरा.. तो ये दुनिया ही मेरी अलग हुआ
करती....

इस रेगिस्तान का समंदर कोई मरीचिका ना होता
और बारिश की बूंदें हम पर गिरा करती...

तुमसे मिलना हमारी चाहतें एक भ्रम ना होता..
तो पहली वर्षा की सौंधी खुशबू यूं नए एहसास का
फूल खिला रही होती।

और ये दुनिया अलग हुआ करती...

तेरे साथ चलना, तेरी बाहें थाम कर एक ख्वाब ना
होता ..
तो कारवां लंबा भी होता और सफर मेरे दिल से
तेरे दिल का ही होता।

ज़्यादा क्या कहूं और क्या ना कहूं..

तेरी आभा की छांव में एक आशियाँ सोचा था...

जो होता तो कांटे भी चुनती और फूल भी...

और ये दुनिया अलग होती।

19. Love and its Ends

They say all good things come to an end..
Why this end is not coming to my heartbreak
trends..

They say Love is a boon if you have been
through..
You rise above heaven if you religiously
pursue..

Though there was no rule book to follow..
I feel I have done everything for thy
lady-love..

We indeed had the most beautiful moments
together..
I ruined it..on breaking up with her, my brute
inside surrendered..

Yes! I was the culprit, I hurt her..broke her
dream heaven forever.
I know her innocence now I shall never be
able to repair..

So..now I am hurt more than ever...cause
crazily I did this a hundred times thereafter..
I questioned myself why I am like this, a devil
creature..
Why she had been loving me since the first
time I met her..

Why do all good feelings have to end?
Why all love stories can't become legends!?

20. Mermaid

I was sitting near the sea shore..when it was a
starry night..
Looking at pearly waves or lodestar that
shines bright..

Seeing my foot traces vanishing under the
tides..
I was lost like a bird from its tribe in mid
flight..

It was then..I saw her..she rose like a mermaid
from the foaming white and dark blue sea...
Her curvature was highlighted with
moonlight..
Her eyes sparkled bright which made me
glee.. ;)

Golden sand clung to her wet body making
her look like a jewel..
Like diamonds from the Greeks have got a
human soul...

The sea behind was becoming a greedy
pervert that night..
it was pacing on the shores to embrace her
tight..
Not only the sea had been vibrant, the winds
were on their flight too..
In the fight to be the first to love her soon..

Her incredible elegance is muse to my poetic
verse..
Can't she be really happening in my known
universe! :) :)....

21. Will you remember me?

What if I die.. will you remember me in a
good way?
I ain't the Allie from "The Notebook",
You ain't Noah anyway...

But..what if I was shy to tell.. that I loved you
terribly unconditionally everyday..
When I was with you on winter days and
nights.. Laugh and cry...

In a li'l span of time during the holiday..!

What if I die.. just like that..with that thing
on my heart, like shades of grey..
In the colorful world.. when we were hanging
out on Sunday.

When I was broke and you were the only ray..
Of hope and happiness..and when I drank
with you at a happy place near some bay...!

We talked day and night like some old school
which may..
Never can be separated whatever it takes on a
judgement day!

What if it was all a hallucination and turning
out to mayday!
And I shall die with the feeling of being fool I
was..on all those days..!

22. Souls prevailed..

In search of Life and passion....
Souls shattered..souls prevailed...

Looking through the window in the hopes of
feeling rain...
Closing arms when in pain...
Gleams of hopes in eyes and cries within....
Rebouncing like a phoenix from the ashes of
its own..
Lighting the vestige of fire in the nerves..
Souls shattered...souls prevailed...

Looking through the darkness in hopes of
daybreak..
Trailing the morning wind in vain...
Gleams of hopes and cries within...
Flying like a falcon to get the win..
Lightning the vestige of fire in the nerves..
Souls shattered ...souls prevailed!

23. Mutual is it?

You don't love me the way I do...
You say you feel what I feel for you...
Straight lies......my darling you throw!
Still..I hold on to you for wishful love..I do..

You say it feels right when I am with you..
But you stay in complete denial for showing
love..
Say! You haven't enlivened? When I run my
fingers onto your beard.. Haven't you..?
Then, why have you been repelling this
impassion and have been so weirdo!

I don't have reasons to love you..my love..
You gave all the reasons in oblige..
We haven't had any of the deal dear.. nor do a
console..
If you could have said it.. you don't or you
do..

Heart would feel lighter as I die..
And this shall be the last time..
Baby! I would be falling in love and only with
you!

PS: Love is a feeling that, if expressed, makes
a world better place, they say.

24. A small wish

In far far away land..lives a small wish...
waiting for you!
She has golden hair strands and looks like a
moon-faced beautiful woman........
sitting on the window balcony...

Her eyes are on the front aisle..looking for
you...
Will you have the courage darling! To embark
on...?
Have you that passion to die upon....
On nothing but having her!

Will your heart sink and rise on sight of her..

And you know life is meaningful for sure..

So dear O! What is the reason to stay
behind..make a wish!
Get to her, take a strive and unite forever..
For life is a myth and your small wish is
real....

25. Pehli mulakaat

Tumhari khushboo se bhari hai meri zindagi
ki raatein aur din..
Tujse milne ko ginti rahi hun har lamha...har
pal chain..

Teri ankhein..wo teri chuan..muje karte hain
bechain!
Teri batein..wo masumiyat...tere kuch na
kehne si mohabbatein..

Teri khushboo dhund rahi hun apne shareer
par..

In hothon ko tere hoton ki talab hai..
Behak rahi hun teri kameez ko apni bahoon
mein rakh kar..

Ye fir wahi October aa chuka jab tujse
mulakat hui thi..
Wo bahut si baat hui thi.. ek sath kai raat yuh
guzar gyi thi..

Tere cigarette, teri whiskey aur teri diwangi
sab mujhe kabool tha..
Us cigarette ki mehak ko aaj bhi miss kiya
karti hun..
Tera jana.. manana bahut jaroori tha..
But.. letting you go everytime is my
unfortunate destiny

26.

When I met him for the first time, he was a
nearós sailor sailing on the pebbly shore...

His eyes had dew and fire and the heart of a
Salvador...
Although his boat was small and pockets were
drained by..
His ardent love for sailing waited for clear sky
and a star to steer by..
He had the chaste desire to own a tall ship to
stride..

Crossing the seven seas, passing the storms
and rough tide..
I found him in the name of "Phaon". Heard of
being blessed by Aphrodite..
At first sight I was love struck by his esoteric
profile..

Our affinity was growing...on the palaces, on
his seas, on my lyrical notes and can't be
hidden..!

Sea was watching us and mayhap be annoyed..
Sea asked the 'Aeolus' to play his weapon on
us..
And Phaon went back to seas denying our
Eros!

And hence they say...there is something
sacred about salt..found only in our tears and
the seas!!!! Nowhere else in the cosmos.

www.ingramcontent.com/pod-product-compliance
Lightning Source LLC
LaVergne TN
LVHW021252200726
843509LV00012B/1653